FROZEN FUN ON A STICK!

Make Your Own Ice Pops is loaded with creative ideas for delicious desserts. Try these flavorful delights—and more!

* STRAWBERRY DAIQUIRI ICE POP
* WATERMELON COCKTAIL ICE POP
* PEPPERMINT CANDY ICE POP
* CARROT-YOGURT ICE POP
* SANGRIA ICE POP
* BANANA ICE POP
* LEMON ICE POP

MAKE YOUR OWN ICE POPS

MAKE YOUR OWN ICE POPS

with Juices, Puddings, Yogurts, Ice Cream and More!

MATHEW TEKULSKY

BERKLEY BOOKS, NEW YORK

MAKE YOUR OWN ICE POPS

A Berkley Book / published by arrangement with
the author

PRINTING HISTORY
Berkley edition / July 1994

ISBN: 0–425–14298–1

BERKLEY®
Berkley Books are published by The Berkley Publishing Group,
200 Madison Avenue, New York, New York 10016.
BERKLEY and the "B" design
are trademarks belonging to Berkley Publishing Corporation.

PRINTED IN THE UNITED STATES OF AMERICA

10 9 8 7 6 5 4 3 2 1

To my sister Jo and my niece Emily—
The Ice-Pop Queens!
and
To my parents,
for buying me all those ice pops when I was a kid!

ACKNOWLEDGMENTS

I would like to thank the following for their generous assistance in the writing of this book: Arrow Plastic Manufacturing Company, James River Corporation, and Tupperware.

Thanks, as always, to my literary agent, Jane Jordan Browne, for her continued support, and to my editor, Hillary Cige, for her great advice.

CONTENTS

MAKE YOUR OWN ICE POPS

CHAPTER ONE

Ice Pops: An Introduction

As a child, I remember sucking on a fudge pop, the delicious chocolate taste of this frozen treat-on-a-stick rushing around in my mouth—sending pleasurable sensations to every corner of my being; and I remember eating many an ice-cream bar when the Good Humor man arrived in my neighborhood with his bells ringing and the dry ice from his portable freezer wafting small, steamy clouds around that magical opening in the side of his truck, from which all good things emanated.

I also remember eating many of those orange-and-vanilla concoctions that sent alternating taste sensations across my mouth—and, of course, I consumed countless grape and cherry flavored ices, those frozen fruit treats that were always sure to satisfy both the taste buds and the thirst.

Indeed, ever since confectioner Harry Burt invented the Good Humor ice-cream bar in 1920, children of all ages have been enjoying the good humors of the mind that have been created by consuming this delectable dessert or snack.

And ever since inventor Frank Epperson left a glass of

lemonade (with a spoon in it by mistake) on a windowsill overnight in 1923—and the lemonade froze to the spoon during the night—people have been consuming a variety of frozen fruit juices (or flavored ices) that appear (until they have melted or been eaten) at the end of a wooden or plastic stick.

With this book, you will be able to bring the magic of these commercially available frozen treats into your own home—and by making your own ice pops, you will not only be able to control the type and amount of the various ingredients that go into your food, you will also be able to achieve a higher quality item than is generally available commercially—for much less money.

From standard fruit juices such as apple, orange, peach, pear, and grape to tropical fruit juices such as coconut, pineapple, papaya, mango, and banana—to berries such as strawberry, raspberry, cranberry, and blueberry—the list of fruits and fruit juices that can be used to make your own ice pops is a long and varied one indeed.

Add ice pops made with watermelon, cantaloupe, and carrot juice—along with ice pops made with sweet items such as peppermint candy, butterscotch, and peanut brittle—and you've got quite a selection of ice-pop recipes from which to choose.

In addition to using juices, blended fruits, and candies in the recipes, you'll also be able to use puddings, yogurts, coffee, tea, nuts, sodas, gelatin, flavor extracts, spices, and various liquors in order to create a wide variety of pops— for just about any occasion.

How about a Tropical Fruit Ice Pop—with its delicious pieces of papaya, strawberry, and banana scattered throughout—on a hot summer afternoon, while you're sitting in a cabana. Or a Raspberry-Chocolate Ice Pop on a warm August evening after a great meal served on your back porch. Or a Maple Ice Pop, enjoyed on a balmy autumn day with the anticipation of the leaves turning in the air.

Maybe you want to enjoy your chocolate pudding in frozen form on a stick, with walnuts added to it; or a cappuccino or a cup of tea in the same frozen form; or some peach yogurt with sprinkles added to it as a frozen dessert on a stick. Whatever your mood and your desire, there should be an ice-pop recipe included somewhere in this book to satisfy you.

Indeed, an ice pop can quench your thirst—as the Grape Punch Ice Pop will do; satisfy your sweet tooth—as the Vanilla-Cherry Soda Pudding Pop will do; or serve as a party favor—as the Banana-Coconut Daiquiri Ice Pop will do.

Want to enjoy the health benefits of drinking fruit and vegetable juices? Try a Peach-Orange Ice Pop, a Blueberry Delight Ice Pop, or a Carrot-Apple Ice Pop—or if you want a real treat, try the surprisingly sweet and exotic Pineapple-Coconut Ice Pop—wow!

Maybe you want to just have fun with your ice pops. Kids of all ages will enjoy swirling chocolate pudding through vanilla pudding, or chocolate syrup through peanut butter, in order to create a pretty, marbled effect.

You can also layer your ice pops by freezing different-colored juices at different times—for example, Concord grape, orange, and apple; or coconut, pineapple, and peach.

You might also want to try layering ice pops that are made with milk or cream as well, by freezing the lower part of the pop first as chocolate milk or cream, and then adding a butterscotch or vanilla-flavored milk or cream on top of the mold and letting this layer freeze. (This turns into the bottom layer of the pop, of course.) The possibilities are endless, as is the variety of flavors and textures that you can enjoy—all in the same pop!

But whichever ice pops you decide to make, there are a few important guidelines that you should follow in order to make the best pops possible—and you should also know a few things about the equipment that you'll need in order to make your pops.

A Word About Equipment

By consulting the Directory at the end of this book, you will find a number of companies listed that manufacture 2- or 3-ounce plastic ice-pop molds, either in sets of four, six, or eight molds.

These molds are very easy to use. Simply fill the mold with your favorite pop mixture and then insert the plastic stick and handle into the mold. Place the molds in the freezer for 1–3 hours or until the pop mixture is hard, then remove the mold from the freezer and remove the stick (along with your pop) from the mold.

To make it easier to remove the stick from the mold, simply place the mold under running water for a few seconds. This will loosen up the edges of the frozen pop mixture. The stick, along with your pop, will then slide easily out of the mold.

You can also use 3- or 5-ounce paper cups and wooden sticks to make your own homemade ice-pop molds. Simply place the pop mixture in the paper cup and place the cup in the freezer.

In order to keep the wooden stick from tipping over while the mixture is still in liquid form, you can either place the stick in the center of the cup when the pop is partially frozen, or you can hold the stick in place by pushing it through a piece of plastic wrap and covering the cup with the rest of the wrap. This will protect your pop and will also prevent ice crystals from forming as it freezes. After the pop is frozen, simply remove the plastic wrap, peel off the paper cup, and enjoy eating your ice pop.

A Word About Fruit

It's a good idea to use fresh fruits that are in season for your ice pops. This way, you'll be using the highest quality oranges and grapefruits in the spring, strawberries and raspberries in the summer, apples and pears in the fall, and tangerines and cranberries in the winter.

Since these fruits (and vegetables) are in large supply, they will be less expensive as well. Therefore, in some of these recipes you may even wish to substitute fruits that are currently abundant, inexpensive, and easy to obtain for some out-of-season fruits.

When blending fresh fruits into your ice-pop mixtures, feel free to blend each one as much or as little as you wish. If you blend your favorite fruits for just a few seconds, you'll end up with small bits of frozen, fresh fruit through- out your pop—which will serve as little treats as you eat the pop. However, if you want a smooth pop, simply blend the mixture for a long enough time so that all of the whole fruit is blended into the liquid. This will also cause more of the fruit's flavor to sink into the entire flavor of the pop.

In general, the more whole fruit that you blend into your ice-pop mixture, the thicker and chunkier your pop will be; conversely, the more juice that you use, the smoother and icier your pop will be.

In the following recipes, I recommend the use of peeled and sliced fresh fruit or fresh fruit juices whenever possi- ble. If frozen fruit is used, it should be 100% pure and unsweetened. In most of these recipes I have not included adding sugars or other sweeteners, since fruit is naturally sweet. If you wish, however, you should feel free to add sugar, honey, or maple syrup to taste.

Indeed, the natural quality of your ice pops is what sets them apart from many commercial products—without artificial sweeteners, emulsifiers, and food colorings, among other items, your juice pops (and your pops made with other ingredients as well) will be as healthy for you as the fresh fruit juices that have become so popular throughout the country in recent years.

So why not get your vitamin C from the orange juice, grapefruit juice, kiwi fruit, or mangoes that you use in your ice pops? Want some potassium—how about blending some banana in with your strawberries and grapes? Need some pectin—make an ice pop with apple juice in it. Want some beta carotene—try a surprisingly sweet ice pop made with carrot juice.

By supplementing your diet with the vitamins and minerals contained in your homemade ice pops, you will not only have an enjoyable taste experience, you will contribute to your own health as well.

A Word About Cream

If you choose to use heavy cream instead of milk in any of these recipes, you may want to whip the cream first and then stir the nuts, candies, fruits, or other ingredients into the whipped cream. This will create the smoothest pop possible using these ingredients and, in addition, the whipped cream will keep these ingredients suspended throughout the mold until the pop mixture freezes.

If you wish, however, you can also stir these ingredients into the heavy cream (or milk) in a dish or bowl (or even in the ice-pop mold itself) and then place the dish in the freezer until the milk or cream is partially frozen (about a half-hour for heavy cream, 1–2 hours for milk or half-and-half). Then simply stir the ingredients around again so that they're well distributed throughout the milk or cream mixture, and then spoon this partially frozen mixture into the popsicle molds. Heavy ingredients such as nuts, candies, and fruits will now remain suspended throughout the pop.

You can also fill the molds first with the milk or cream and then press the extra ingredients down into the mold when the milk or cream is partially frozen. Be sure to leave enough room at the top of each mold to do this, or the milk or cream will overflow when too many of these extra ingredients have been added to the mold.

Ice pops made with milk or half-and-half will be icier than those made with heavy cream, but they'll be refreshing in their own way—and will contain far fewer calories and fat than the pops made with heavy cream.

Remember that the more often you stir your partially frozen pop mixtures, the smoother your pops will be since by stirring you are breaking down the ice crystals in the milk or cream mixture into smaller components.

When using whipped cream, be sure to fill the popsicle mold well and be sure there are no air pockets around the stick. This will allow for the pop mixture to adhere as well as possible to the stick.

Stirring Your Pop Mixture

Sometimes blended fruit such as strawberries and raspberries rise to the top of the mold. If you stir the mixture around when it is partially frozen, you'll be able to spread this whole fruit around the pop more easily. By stirring the pop around at this time, you'll be making it even smoother by breaking down the ice crystals even further.

There are a number of other circumstances under which you may need to stir the pop mixture around when it's partially frozen in order to make sure that certain ingredients don't sink to the bottom of the mold, or rise to the top. In these instances, you can either stir the mixture around while it's in the mold or you can place the mixture in a separate container and fill the molds after the mixture has been partially frozen and stirred.

For instance, the pulp from fresh orange and apple juice will tend to separate and rise to the top of the mold, while bottled or frozen concentrated juices that have water added to them may sink to the bottom of the mold when mixed with fresh juices.

Similarly, while marshmallows and pieces of cantaloupe rise to the top of the liquid pop mixture in the mold, unsalted roasted peanuts and pieces of peppermint candy will sink to the bottom of the mold. But while chopped pecans, walnuts, hazelnuts, and almonds float to the top of the mold, most ground almonds will sink to the bottom, while about half of ground pecans, walnuts, and hazelnuts will. (The rest remain in suspension or float on top.) In addition, ground spices may sink to the bottom of the mold, so be sure to give them a little stir when the pop is partially frozen, if necessary.

By becoming familiar with the various ingredients that you'll be using to make your ice pops, you'll soon discover the different properties that they have and how to best make use of each ingredient.

A Note on Ingredients

1. The recipes that are included in this book are comprised of 12-ounce batches—designed to fit into either six 2-ounce plastic ice-pop molds or four 3-ounce plastic ice-pop molds or paper cups. If you wish to make more (or fewer) servings of these recipes, simply multiply (or divide) the amount of each ingredient to provide for the number of ice pops that you wish to make.

Certain ingredients such as honey, maple syrup, and various flavor extracts do not add significantly enough to the volume of each ice pop to warrant subtracting an equal amount of some other ingredient—so although mathematically the volume of ingredients will exceed two ounces per pop, in reality the volume will be so close to two ounces per pop as to be insignificant.

When blending or stirring in certain ingredients like ground nuts, or fresh or shredded coconut, some shrinkage in volume may occur, so compensate for this by adding an equal amount of juice, milk, or whole fruit, if necessary.

2. In addition to using juices in the following recipes, please feel free to use as many blended fruits, berries, and melons as you wish. You can even make a single ice pop out of such blended items as raspberries, kiwi fruit, bananas, and strawberries, if you so desire.

When fresh, frozen, or canned fruit is used in the following recipes, it should be peeled (if necessary) and sliced or chopped into small pieces before placing the mixture into the blender.

When whole fruit is blended into your pop mixture instead of that fruit's juice, the resulting pop will be thicker and harder than if you had just used the juice. Therefore, the more whole fruit that is blended into your pops, the more sugar and liquor you'll be able to use before the frozen pop becomes too soft or melts too quickly after it's taken out of the freezer.

For juices that are hard to find or require a juice extractor to prepare—such as strawberry or raspberry juice, watermelon and cantaloupe juice, or kiwi, papaya, and mango juice—I've included the whole fruit in the recipe. Please feel free to substitute an equal amount of the appropriate juice for these ingredients.

If a certain fresh fruit or fruit juice isn't available, you may wish to use a bottled or canned nectar such as those for peach, strawberry, apricot, papaya, or mango. These products may have corn syrup or other sweeteners added to them, which may cause your ice pop to turn out softer than it would if you used unsweetened fruit juice. So you may wish to use a little bit less of these nectars, and a little more fresh whole fruit or fruit juice with the other ingredients in these recipes.

Similarly, I use unsweetened cranberry juice in these recipes, but if this is not available, a bottled or canned cranberry "cocktail" can be used. Again, since this product has corn syrup in it, you may wish to use a little bit less of this product and a little bit more of another ingredient in order to achieve the hardest pop possible using these ingredients.

3. In the recipes that use milk, I suggest using 2% lowfat milk. However, please feel free to substitute plain nonfat or lowfat yogurt, nonfat milk, 1% lowfat milk, whole milk, half-and-half, or heavy cream (or any combination of any of these ingredients) for the 2% lowfat milk in any of these recipes, depending on your taste.

If you use plain nonfat or lowfat yogurt instead of the milk, you can stir ingredients such as nuts, candies, and fruits into the yogurt and the yogurt will keep these ingredients suspended throughout the mold until the pop mixture freezes. (Using yogurt instead of milk will result in a thicker pop, but one that may require some extra sweetening as yogurt is naturally a bit sour.)

4. When not otherwise specified, regular granulated sugar or confectioners' sugar (or other sweeteners, such as

honey and brown sugar) can be added to any of these recipes, depending on your taste. Most of the pops taste sweet enough without any sugar added at all. It's up to you.

5. In the recipes using grape juice, I suggest using either white or Concord grape juice, which are easily available in bottled or canned form. However, if you have your own juice extractor, you may wish to use Thompson seedless or red grape juice for the same recipes.

6. Nectarines can be substituted for peaches in the recipes.

7. There are a number of different commercial products that are called coconut juice or coconut milk. Any of these will suffice, and you may wish to use chopped fresh coconut instead of packaged shredded coconut (sweetened or unsweetened). Sweetened shredded coconut will make your ice pop substantially sweeter, but not substantially softer since this is a solid item.

8. In the following recipes, watermelon and cantaloupe pieces should be used without the rind; and watermelon pieces should be seeded as well. Honeydew melon or other similar melons can be substituted for (or combined with) cantaloupe.

9. Ice pops with nuts in them can be made using chopped, sliced, or ground nuts. If you roast chopped or sliced nuts in the oven for 5–10 minutes at 350°F (or ground nuts for 3–5 minutes), you will bring out the flavor of the nuts more and you'll also have toastier nuts in your pop. All pop mixtures with nuts (except those with whipped cream or yogurt) should be stirred when the mixture is partially frozen in order to disperse the nuts throughout the pop and make sure that none of the nuts remain at the top or sink to the bottom of the mold.

10. Commercially prepared frozen yogurt can be substituted for ice cream in any of these recipes.

11. You may wish to add such ingredients as protein powders or other nutritional supplements to your ice pops. While powders such as these will make your pops grainier than normal, they add a richness and variety that will also contribute to your health. When using any supplemental powders, be sure to stir the pop around when it's partially frozen to make sure that the juice and the powder don't separate and that the powder is thoroughly mixed into the pop.

Tips for Making the Best Ice Pops

Here are a few tips for making the best ice pops possible:

1. Be sure not to fill the plastic mold or paper cup up to the very top, or it may overflow, as the mixture will expand just a bit as it freezes. But be sure to fill the mold up high enough on the stick to create a large enough area for the pop mixture to get a good hold. In most cases, about a ¼-inch gap at the top of the mold or cup will be large enough to serve both purposes. (You should leave about ½ inch of space at the top of the mold for ice pops made with sodas, as sodas expand more than other ingredients when frozen and will cause quite a mess if they overflow.)

2. Be sure to leave the mold or cup in the freezer long enough for the pop to freeze well—anywhere from 1–3 hours for a regular juice pop to 6–8 hours for a milk- or cream-based pop, to even longer for pops with liquor or lots of sugar in them. This is because the more cream, sugar, or liquor that you have in your ice pops, the longer they will take to freeze and the softer the pops will be.

3. When making layered pops using liquid ingredients that need to be frozen at separate times, be sure not to fill plastic molds so high that the stick gets stuck in the first layer. Then you won't be able to get the stick out to pour in your next ingredient. So by all means make layered pops, but be aware of the limitations of this technique. For instance, you may wish to make a few thin layers at the top of the pop (i.e. the bottom of the mold), until you reach the tip of the stick; then fill in the rest of the mold with liquid after the lower layers are frozen. This way, the stick will fit into the mold and won't be pushed up over the top by meeting a layer of frozen liquid. (When using paper cups to make your ice pops, you can make your layers as high as you wish, since the paper cups don't have tops like the plastic molds do. In this case, simply place the stick into the first layer, and then fill up the rest of the cup with as many layers as you want after that.) With thicker ingredients such as yogurts and puddings, layered pops can be prepared all at the same time, since these ingredients will rest on top of each other without mixing together before they're frozen.

4. Please feel free to use your own creativity and make up the ice-pop recipes that you like best—and most of all, have fun and enjoy eating your own homemade ice pops!

CHAPTER TWO

Ice Pops Made
With Standard Fruit Juices

In addition to the following recipes, feel free to make your own ice pops using single standard fruit juices such as apple, orange, peach, pear, apricot, grapefruit, grape, lemon and lime (you'll need to add some sugar to these!), and any combinations thereof. Enjoy!

FRUIT PUNCH ICE POP

A great combination of citrus juices (with a little bit of pineapple thrown in for good measure), this pop is perfect for a sunny summer afternoon.

6 oz. orange juice
3 oz. grapefruit juice
1 oz. lemon juice
2 oz. pineapple juice

Stir all the ingredients together and pour this mixture into the molds. Place the molds in the freezer.

APPLE PUNCH ICE POP

If you blend the strawberries for just a few moments you'll get a frozen strawberry treat every now and then throughout this dark purple, punchy pop.

6 oz. apple juice
2 oz. orange juice
2 oz. strawberries, sliced
2 oz. Concord grape juice
⅛ tsp. ground cinnamon
⅛ tsp. ground cloves

Mix all the ingredients in a blender for 10–15 seconds, or until smooth. Pour this mixture into the molds and place the molds in the freezer.

Variations: Substitute 2 ounces peeled and sliced cantaloupe (or honeydew melon) for the strawberries; or use 1 ounce of either melon and 1 ounce strawberries; or use ⅔ ounce each of strawberries, cantaloupe, and honeydew melon in order to create red, orange, and light green pieces in this pop. Proceed as directed above.

GRAPE PUNCH ICE POP

This dark, reddish-purple pop has a delicious tang to it from the lemon juice, and actually tastes like a sangria— but without the wine.

6 oz. Concord grape juice
2 oz. orange juice
2 oz. lemon juice
2 oz. grapefruit juice

   Stir all the ingredients together and pour this mixture into the molds. Place the molds in the freezer.

GRAPE TEA ICE POP

The light, flowery flavor of the hibiscus tea makes this light pink pop taste like a grapevine or an apple orchard, depending on which variation you use.

6 oz. white grape juice
6 oz. freshly brewed hibiscus (or another herb) tea

Stir the grape juice into the hibiscus tea. Pour this mixture into the molds and place the molds in the freezer.

Variations: For a reddish-purple pop that tastes more strongly of grape, substitute 6 ounces Concord grape juice for the white grape juice. For an *Apple Tea Ice Pop*, substitute 6 ounces apple juice for the grape juice. Proceed as directed above.

PEACH-ORANGE ICE POP

Peaches and oranges mix beautifully in this orange-colored pop.

8 oz. peaches, peeled and sliced
4 oz. orange juice

Mix the ingredients in a blender for 10–15 seconds, or until smooth. Pour this mixture into the molds and place the molds in the freezer.

PEACH-VANILLA ICE POP

This fantastic pop both looks and tastes like frozen eggnog on a stick—and it's easy to bite through as well!

6 oz. peaches, peeled and sliced
6 oz. vanilla ice cream
¾ tsp. almond extract
¾ tsp. ground nutmeg

Mix all the ingredients in a blender for 10–15 seconds, or until smooth. Spoon this mixture into the molds and place the molds in the freezer.

19

APPLE-STRAWBERRY ICE POP

A pinkish pop with a white tint in it from the coconut juice, this one adds an exotic accent to the taste of two common fruits.

4 oz. apple juice
4 oz. strawberries, sliced
2 oz. coconut juice
2 oz. papaya, peeled and sliced

Mix all the ingredients in a blender for 10–15 seconds, or until smooth. Pour this mixture into the molds and place the molds in the freezer.

ORANGE SMOOTHIE ICE POP

This mostly orange-strawberry tasting pop is made all the richer by the addition of the other three fruits—like a frozen smoothie on a stick.

6 oz. orange juice
2 oz. strawberries, sliced
2 oz. raspberries
1 oz. papaya, peeled and sliced
1 oz. kiwi fruit, peeled and sliced

    Mix all the ingredients in a blender for 10–15 seconds, or until smooth. Pour this mixture into the molds and place the molds in the freezer.

APPLE SMOOTHIE ICE POP

With the banana and strawberry flavors enhancing the predominant apple flavor of this light pink pop, this is a smoothie that can't be beat.

6 oz. apple juice
2 oz. banana, peeled and sliced
2 oz. strawberries, sliced
1 oz. pear, peeled and sliced
1 oz. papaya, peeled and sliced

Mix all the ingredients in a blender for 10–15 seconds, or until smooth. Pour this mixture into the molds and place the molds in the freezer.

PEAR SMOOTHIE ICE POP

If you have a juice extractor try to use fresh pear and peach juice for this ice pop—otherwise, use an equal amount of peeled and sliced pieces of fresh peaches and pears.

6 oz. pear juice
2 oz. peach juice
2 oz. apple juice
1 oz. strawberries, sliced
1 oz. banana, peeled and sliced

Mix all the ingredients in a blender for 10–15 seconds, or until smooth. Pour this mixture into the molds and place the molds in the freezer.

MIXED FRUIT ICE POP

If you are having a party or a get-together on a summer evening, this orangish pop will be a real hit with its well-balanced combination of fruity tastes—an ambrosia pop!

2 oz. apple juice
2 oz. orange juice
2 oz. strawberries, sliced
2 oz. pineapple juice
2 oz. peaches, peeled and sliced
2 oz. banana, peeled and sliced

Mix all the ingredients in a blender for 10–15 seconds, or until smooth. Pour this mixture into the molds and place the molds in the freezer.

APPLE-WALNUT ICE POP

A milky-white pop with dark brown pieces of walnut in it. The apple-flavored milk is a special treat.

5 oz. milk
5 oz. apple juice
2 oz. chopped walnuts

Stir the apple juice and the walnuts into the milk in a bowl and place the bowl in the freezer for 1–2 hours, or until the mixture is partially frozen. Stir the mixture again to spread the walnuts evenly throughout the milk and spoon this mixture into the molds. Place the molds in the freezer.

GRAPE-RAISIN ICE POP

This light purple pop has a great grape-flavored, milky taste that is complemented by the raisins that are spread throughout the pop.

5 oz. milk
5 oz. Concord grape juice
2 oz. raisins

Stir the grape juice and the raisins into the milk in a bowl and place the bowl in the freezer for 1–2 hours, or until the mixture is partially frozen. Stir the mixture again to spread the raisins evenly throughout the milk and spoon this mixture into the molds. Place the molds in the freezer.

LEMON ICE POP

A pale yellow pop, this one tastes like the filling of a lemon chiffon pie—vanilla, with the tart taste of lemon.

  2 oz. lemon juice
12 oz. vanilla pudding

Stir the juice into the pudding and spoon this mixture into the molds. Place the molds in the freezer.

Variation: For a *Lime Ice Pop*, substitute 2 ounces lime juice for the lemon juice. Proceed as directed above.

ORANGE ICE POP

This pop is like having an orange sherbet on a stick.

10 oz. orange juice
  2 oz. lemon juice

Stir the ingredients together and pour the mixture into the molds. Place the molds in the freezer.

PEACH ICE POP

With its strong peach flavor, this pop is like having a taste of Georgia on a stick.

9 oz. peach juice
2 oz. apricots, peeled and sliced
1 oz. lemon juice

Mix all the ingredients in a blender for 10–15 seconds, or until smooth. Pour this mixture into the molds and place the molds in the freezer.

CIDER ICE POP

Add the tang of lemon to your apple cider and you have a perfect ice pop for a warm Indian summer day.

10 oz. apple cider
2 oz. lemon juice

Stir the ingredients together and pour the mixture into the molds. Place the molds in the freezer.

ORANGE-MILK ICE POP

*To make your own homemade "Milksicle," simply follow
the instructions below for this delicious pop—then enjoy
alternating your licks and bites between the orange juice
and the sweet milk (a great treat when you finish each
pop). Note: It is necessary to freeze the milk and orange
(or tangerine) juice separately with this pop, because if
you mix the milk and orange juice together when these
ingredients are both in liquid form, the milk will curdle.
However, if you whip 6 ounces of heavy cream (instead
of milk) along with the sugar, you can pour 1 ounce of
the orange juice into each mold and fill the rest up with
the whipped cream; then place the molds in the freezer.
With this technique (your own homemade "Creamsicle"),
the whipped cream will rest on top of the orange juice, and
therefore the juice won't curdle.*

6 oz. orange juice
1 oz. sugar
6 oz. milk

Pour 1 ounce of the orange juice into each mold and
place the molds in the freezer until the orange juice is
frozen. Stir the sugar into the milk and fill the rest of
each mold up with this mixture. Place the molds back in
the freezer.

Variation: For a *Tangerine-Milk Ice Pop,* substitute 6
ounces of tangerine juice for the orange juice. Proceed as
directed above.

GRAPE-GELATIN ICE POP I

The great thing about using gelatin in your ice pops is that they don't drip—and they taste great, too! In addition to grape, you can use any of your favorite flavored gelatins all by themselves to make a great pop.

8 oz. grape-flavored gelatin
4 oz. canned fruit cocktail, drained

Prepare the gelatin as you normally would by following the package instructions. Place the gelatin in a bowl in the freezer until the gelatin is partially thickened (about 20 minutes). Remove the gelatin from the freezer and stir the fruit cocktail into the gelatin. Spoon this mixture into the molds and place the molds in the freezer.

Variation: Substitute 4 ounces of your favorite fruit (peeled and sliced, if necessary)—such as cantaloupe or pear—for the fruit cocktail. Proceed as directed above.

GRAPE-GELATIN ICE POP II

By using unflavored gelatin and unsweetened fruit juice you will be able to make your own homemade gelatin pop that you can customize to satisfy your own taste requirements. Please feel free to use whichever fruit juice you like best with this recipe. (Note: This recipe will make two extra 2-ounce pops.)

16 oz. grape juice
1 tbs. unflavored gelatin

Place 8 ounces of the grape juice in a bowl. Sprinkle the gelatin onto the juice and let the mixture stand for a minute. Heat the remaining juice to boiling and pour the hot juice over the cold juice mixture. Stir the mixture for about five minutes, or until all of the gelatin is dissolved. Spoon this mixture into the molds and place the molds in the freezer.

FRUIT COCKTAIL ICE POP I

Fans of frozen yogurt will love this pop, with its small pieces of peaches, pears, grapes, pineapples, and maraschino cherries that are spread throughout. Since the yogurt already has sugar in it be sure to drain the syrup well from the fruit cocktail.

6 oz. canned fruit cocktail, drained
6 oz. peach (or orange) yogurt

Stir the fruit cocktail into the yogurt and spoon this mixture into the molds. Place the molds in the freezer.

Variation: For a tarter pop, substitute 6 ounces of plain yogurt for the flavored yogurt. Proceed as directed above.

FRUIT COCKTAIL ICE POP II

By adding the tangy lemon juice to the sweet fruit cocktail, you end up with a refreshing yet pungent treat.

 2 oz. lemon juice
10 oz. canned fruit cocktail, with syrup

Stir the lemon juice into the fruit cocktail. Spoon this mixture into the molds and place the molds in the freezer.

Variation: Substitute 6 ounces of orange juice and 6 ounces of drained fruit cocktail for the lemon juice and fruit cocktail with syrup. Proceed as directed above.

PLUM ICE POP

This great pop is like having your own homemade plum ice cream on a stick.

6 oz. plums, peeled and sliced
6 oz. vanilla ice cream

Mix the ingredients in a blender for 10–15 seconds, or until smooth. Spoon this mixture into the molds and place the molds in the freezer.

APPLE-ORANGE ICE POP

A simple combination of tastes, this pop takes our two favorite fruits and blends them together beautifully.

6 oz. apple juice
6 oz. orange juice

Stir the ingredients together and pour this mixture into the molds. Place the molds in the freezer.

Variations: For a stronger apple taste with a hint of orange, use 8 ounces of apple juice and 4 ounces of orange juice. Proceed as directed above.

For a spicier pop, you may wish to stir ¾ teaspoon of ground cinnamon into either pop mixture before filling the molds.

ORANGE-GRENADINE ICE POP

An orange-colored pop with a hint of red in it, the red reflects the sweet taste of the grenadine.

11 oz. orange juice
1 oz. grenadine

Stir the ingredients together and pour this mixture into the molds. Place the molds in the freezer.

Variation: For a *Grapefruit-Grenadine Ice Pop*, substitute 11 ounces of grapefruit juice for the orange juice. Proceed as directed above.

APPLESAUCE-CINNAMON ICE POP

Tiny brown bits of cinnamon are visible throughout this pop—which tastes like a fall day.

¾ tsp. ground cinnamon
12 oz. unsweetened applesauce

Stir the cinnamon into the applesauce and spoon this mixture into the molds. Place the molds in the freezer.

APPLESAUCE-STRAWBERRY ICE POP

*The strawberries in this pop complement the applesauce—
as do the bananas when added.*

  2 oz. strawberries, sliced
10 oz. unsweetened applesauce

Stir the strawberries into the applesauce and spoon this
mixture into the molds. Place the molds in the freezer.

Variations: Substitute 1 ounce of peeled and sliced
banana for 1 ounce of the strawberries and proceed as
directed above. Feel free to add any combination of fresh
fruits that you wish to this pop.

CHAPTER THREE

Ice Pops Made
With Tropical Fruit Juices

In addition to the following recipes, feel free to make your own ice pops using single tropical fruit juices such as coconut, pineapple, papaya, kiwi, mango, and any combinations thereof.

KIWI ICE POP

On a hot day, this beautiful olive-green ice pop will give you a great taste of New Zealand and the tropics put together.

2 oz. honey
6 oz. coconut juice
6 oz. kiwi fruit, peeled and sliced

Stir the honey into the coconut juice until the honey is dissolved. Add the kiwi fruit to the coconut juice and blend this mixture for 10–15 seconds, or until smooth. Pour the mixture into the molds and place the molds in the freezer.

PAPAYA SODA ICE POP

A light yellow pop with lots of soft, crunchy ice crystals from the carbonated water, this one is like having a papaya soda on a stick.

3 oz. papaya juice
3 oz. white grape juice
1½ oz. pineapple juice
4½ oz. carbonated water

Stir all the ingredients together and pour this mixture into the molds. Place the molds in the freezer.

MANGO-GRAPE ICE POP

This purplish-orange pop is really neat with its tasty little bits of frozen mango in it.

6 oz. mango, peeled and sliced
6 oz. Concord grape juice

Mix the ingredients in a blender for 10–15 seconds, or until smooth. Pour this mixture into the molds and place the molds in the freezer.

Variations: For a *Mango-Apple Ice Pop*, substitute 6 ounces of apple juice for the grape juice. Proceed as directed above.

To add the taste of peach to these pops, substitute 3 ounces of grape or apple juice along with 3 ounces of peach juice (or peeled and sliced peaches) for the 6 ounces of grape or apple juice. Proceed as directed above.

PAPAYA-KIWI ICE POP

This light, olive-green pop contains bits of banana and bits of papaya in it—a great exotic frozen treat!

4 oz. papaya, peeled and sliced
4 oz. kiwi fruit, peeled and sliced
2 oz. apple juice
2 oz. banana, peeled and sliced

Mix all the ingredients in a blender for 10–15 seconds, or until smooth. Pour this mixture into the molds and place the molds in the freezer.

TROPICAL FRUIT ICE POP

This pinkish-orange pop contains a hint of white from the coconut juice, and tasty pieces of papaya, strawberry, and banana throughout—delicious!

2 oz. papaya, peeled and sliced
2 oz. coconut juice
4 oz. pineapple juice
2 oz. strawberries, sliced
2 oz. banana, peeled and sliced

Mix all the ingredients in a blender for 10–15 seconds, or until smooth. Pour this mixture into the molds and place the molds in the freezer.

Variation: Substitute 2 ounces raspberries for the strawberries. Proceed as directed above.

PINEAPPLE SMOOTHIE ICE POP

For a tropical summer treat, enjoy the tangy taste of this pineapple pop as it's complemented by these other delicious fruits.

6 oz. pineapple juice
2 oz. orange juice
2 oz. white grape juice
1 oz. strawberries, sliced
1 oz. banana, peeled and sliced

Mix all the ingredients in a blender for 10–15 seconds, or until smooth. Pour this mixture into the molds and place the molds in the freezer.

BANANA-PEACH ICE POP

The hint of peach taste in this pop gives the banana just the richness that it needs.

6 oz. banana, peeled and sliced
3 oz. peaches, peeled and sliced
3 oz. vanilla yogurt

Mix all the ingredients in a blender for 10–15 seconds, or until smooth. Pour this mixture into the molds and place the molds in the freezer.

COCONUT ICE POP

A light pinkish pop with a hint of white from the coconut juice, this pop'll make you feel like you're on a Caribbean island.

4 oz. coconut juice
2 oz. apple juice
2 oz. papaya, peeled and sliced
2 oz. strawberries, sliced
2 oz. banana, peeled and sliced

Mix all the ingredients in a blender for 10–15 seconds, or until smooth. Pour this mixture into the molds and place the molds in the freezer.

BANANA-HONEY ICE POP

This smooth-tasting pop has a predominant banana flavor with a rich aftertaste of milk and honey.

3 oz. milk
8 oz. banana, peeled and sliced
1 oz. honey

Mix all the ingredients in a blender for 10–15 seconds, or until smooth. Pour this mixture into the molds and place the molds in the freezer.

COCONUT-MARSHMALLOW ICE POP

This white pop allows you to taste first the coconut and then the marshmallows, and then back to the coconut taste again—and so on!

12 oz. coconut juice
3 oz. marshmallows, sliced

Mix the ingredients in a blender for 10–15 seconds, or until smooth. Pour this mixture into the molds and place the molds in the freezer. When the mixture is partially frozen, stir the mixture in order to distribute the marshmallows evenly throughout the pop.

Variation: For a creamier pop, substitute 6 ounces of half-and-half for 6 ounces of the coconut juice. Proceed as directed above.

PINEAPPLE-MARSHMALLOW ICE POP

If you want all the cherries at the tip of this pop, just let them sink to the bottom of the mold and leave them there— when you pull the pop out of the mold, the cherries will now be on top.

12 oz. pineapple juice
 3 oz. marshmallows, sliced
 1 oz. maraschino cherries, sliced

Mix the pineapple juice and the marshmallows in a blender for 10–15 seconds, or until smooth. Pour this mixture into the molds, add about 1 teaspoon of cherry bits to each mold, and place the molds in the freezer. When the mixture is partially frozen, stir the mixture in order to distribute the marshmallows and cherry bits evenly throughout the pop.

PAPAYA-MILK ICE POP

This light orange pop is so sweet, you don't even need sugar in it!

6 oz. milk
6 oz. papaya, peeled and sliced

Mix the ingredients in a blender for 10–15 seconds, or until smooth. Pour this mixture into the molds and place the molds in the freezer.

Variation: For a *Mango-Milk Ice Pop*, substitute 6 ounces of peeled and sliced mango for the papaya. Proceed as directed above.

BANANA ICE POP

The riper the banana, the better this pop will taste. When it's frozen, the banana will turn a darker color, but this has no effect on the banana's taste or freshness.

12 oz. banana, peeled and sliced

Mix the banana in a blender for 10–15 seconds, or until smooth. Spoon the banana into the molds and place the molds in the freezer.

PINEAPPLE-COCONUT ICE POP

A simple idea, but does this pop pack a taste punch—a great tropical treat!

6 oz. pineapple juice
6 oz. coconut juice

Stir the ingredients together and pour this mixture into the molds. Place the molds in the freezer.

ROOT BEER-COCONUT ICE POP

An unlikely combination of ingredients, you'll be surprised at how good this pop will taste.

6 oz. root beer
6 oz. coconut juice

Stir the ingredients together and pour this mixture into the molds. Place the molds in the freezer. When the mixture is partially frozen, stir the mixture in order to distribute the coconut juice evenly throughout the pop.

CHAPTER FOUR

Ice Pops Made
With Berry Juices

In addition to the following recipes, feel free to make your own ice pops using single berry juices such as strawberry, raspberry, cranberry, cherry, blueberry, and any combinations thereof.

STRAWBERRY-STRAWBERRY
ICE POP

No matter which fruit you choose, for a double-flavor dose of your favorite ice cream, this pop is sure to hit the spot.

6 oz. strawberries, sliced
6 oz. strawberry ice cream

Mix the ingredients in a blender for 10–15 seconds, or until smooth. Pour this mixture into the molds and place the molds in the freezer.

CRANBERRY-GRAPE ICE POP

Whether you make a cranberry-colored pop with the white grape juice or a purple pop with the Concord grape juice, you'll find that the grape juice sweetens the cranberry juice naturally and creates a great punchy taste.

6 oz. cranberry juice
6 oz. white (or Concord) grape juice

Stir the ingredients together and pour this mixture into the molds. Place the molds in the freezer.

Variations: For a *Cranberry-Apple Ice Pop*, substitute 6 ounces of apple juice for the grape juice. Proceed as directed above.

For a *Cranberry-Raspberry Ice Pop*, substitute 6 ounces of raspberries for the grape juice. Add 1 ounce of sugar and mix all the ingredients in a blender for 10–15 seconds, or until smooth. Pour this mixture into the molds and place the molds in the freezer. When the mixture is partially frozen, stir the mixture in order to distribute the raspberries evenly throughout the pop.

RASPBERRY ICE POP

The addition of raspberries to any ice pop creates a delicious taste sensation—and a beautiful, rich red color to enjoy.

6 oz. raspberries
3 oz. apple juice
3 oz. white (or Concord) grape juice

Mix all the ingredients in a blender for 10–15 seconds, or until smooth. Pour this mixture into the molds and place the molds in the freezer. When the mixture is partially frozen, stir the mixture in order to distribute the raspberries evenly throughout the pop.

Variation: Substitute 6 ounces of cranberry juice for the raspberries. Stir all the ingredients together and pour this mixture into the molds. Place the molds in the freezer.

CRANBERRY-TEA ICE POP

If you use dried hibiscus flowers to make the tea (watch the flowers expand as they soak up the water!), you can have some fun while you make this pop—which is sweet from the honey and light from the hibiscus tea. This one's a perfect refreshment for a hot summer evening on a veranda or in a gazebo.

6 oz. cranberry juice
1 oz. honey
6 oz. freshly brewed hibiscus (or another herb) tea

Stir the cranberry juice and the honey into the hibiscus tea until the honey is dissolved. Pour this mixture into the molds and place the molds in the freezer.

CRANBERRY-GRAPE TEA ICE POP

Since not that much grape juice is used proportionally in this recipe, you may want to stir 1 ounce of honey into the pop mixture before pouring the mixture into the molds. This will sweeten your pop a little bit more than it is already—as it is, the pop has a tangy and sweet taste from the cranberry and grape juices respectively.

4 oz. cranberry juice
2 oz. white (or Concord) grape juice
6 oz. freshly brewed hibiscus (or another herb) tea

Stir the cranberry and grape juices into the hibiscus tea. Pour this mixture into the molds and place the molds in the freezer.

STRAWBERRY-BANANA ICE POP

This light, pinkish-red pop is thick and fleshy—like having a frozen fruit bar on a stick.

6 oz. strawberries, sliced
3 oz. banana, peeled and sliced
3 oz. orange juice

Mix all the ingredients in a blender for 10–15 seconds, or until smooth. Pour this mixture into the molds and place the molds in the freezer.

Variation: For a *Raspberry-Banana Ice Pop*, substitute 6 ounces of raspberries for the strawberries. Proceed as directed above.

STRAWBERRY-WATERMELON
ICE POP

The watermelon in this pop makes you feel as if you're on a picnic—and the strawberries are a great complement to the watermelon taste.

6 oz. strawberries, sliced
6 oz. watermelon, sliced

Mix the ingredients in a blender for 10–15 seconds, or until smooth. Pour this mixture into the molds and place the molds in the freezer.

Variations: For a stronger strawberry taste with a hint of watermelon, use 8 ounces of strawberries and 4 ounces of watermelon. Proceed as directed above.

For a *Raspberry-Watermelon Ice Pop*, substitute raspberries for strawberries in the recipes listed above.

BLUEBERRY-VANILLA ICE POP

Not only does this dark purple pop give you the great taste of blueberries, but the vanilla extract adds a rich aftertaste to the flavor—like having your own homemade blueberry ice cream on a stick!

6 oz. blueberries
6 oz. vanilla ice cream
¾ tsp. vanilla extract

Mix all the ingredients in a blender for 10–15 seconds, or until smooth. Pour this mixture into the molds and place the molds in the freezer.

BLUEBERRY DELIGHT ICE POP

This dark purple pop with its bits of banana and peach in it is as tasty as it looks—making the great flavor of blueberries even better.

6 oz. blueberries
2 oz. apple juice
2 oz. peaches, peeled and sliced
2 oz. banana, peeled and sliced

Mix all the ingredients in a blender for 10–15 seconds, or until smooth. Pour this mixture into the molds and place the molds in the freezer.

Variation: For a *Blueberry Delight Mint Ice Pop*, add ⅜ teaspoon of mint extract to the pop mixture listed above before placing the mixture in the blender. Proceed as directed above.

RASPBERRY SMOOTHIE ICE POP

This bright pink pop, with its bits of banana and strawberry in it, is like having a tropical smoothie on a stick.

6 oz. raspberries
2 oz. apple juice
1 oz. pineapple juice
1 oz. coconut juice
2 oz. banana, peeled and sliced

Mix all the ingredients in a blender for 10–15 seconds, or until smooth. Pour this mixture into the molds and place the molds in the freezer.

RASPBERRY-CHOCOLATE ICE POP

What can you say about the taste of raspberries and chocolate together—incredible!

 4 oz. raspberries
 6 oz. plain yogurt
 2 oz. chocolate syrup
1⅓ oz. honey

  Mix all the ingredients in a blender for 10–15 seconds, or until smooth. Pour this mixture into the molds and place the molds in the freezer.

  Variation: For a *Strawberry-Chocolate Ice Pop*, substitute 4 ounces of strawberries for the raspberries. Proceed as directed above.

BLUEBERRY-YOGURT ICE POP

You get a double blueberry one-two punch with this pop.

6 oz. blueberries
6 oz. blueberry yogurt

Stir the blueberries into the yogurt and spoon this mixture into the molds. Place the molds in the freezer.

Variations: Substitute 6 ounces of your favorite fruit and 6 ounces of your favorite fruit yogurt of the same fruit (e.g., strawberries and strawberry yogurt, raspberries and raspberry yogurt, peaches and peach yogurt) for the blueberries and blueberry yogurt. Proceed as directed above.

CHERRY-MILK ICE POP

If you substitute strawberries or peaches for cherries with this ice pop, it's like having the frozen icing from a strawberry or peach shortcake on a stick—delicious!

6 oz. milk
1 oz. sugar
6 oz. cherries, sliced

Mix all the ingredients in a blender for 10–15 seconds, or until smooth. Pour this mixture into the molds and place the molds in the freezer.

Variations: Substitute 3 ounces each of two fruits (e.g., strawberry-cherry or blueberry-peach), or any combination of fruits thereof. Proceed as directed above.

If you wish to include the great taste of maple syrup in any of these recipes, simply substitute 1 ounce of maple syrup for the sugar and proceed as directed above.

CRANBERRY-YOGURT ICE POP

You may want to add a little bit of extra sugar to this tart, dark pink pop.

4 oz. plain yogurt
1 oz. sugar
8 oz. cranberry juice

Stir the yogurt and the sugar into the cranberry juice until all the ingredients are mixed together well. Pour this mixture into the molds and place the molds in the freezer.

RASPBERRY-LEMON ICE POP

This raspberry-red pop is both tangy and sweet at the same time.

9 oz. raspberries
3 oz. lemon juice
1 oz. sugar

Mix all the ingredients in a blender for 10–15 seconds, or until smooth. Pour this mixture into the molds and place the molds in the freezer.

STRAWBERRY-CRANBERRY ICE POP

Whether you use strawberries or raspberries in this ice pop, you're sure to get a red one that's full of berry power.

6 oz. strawberries, sliced
6 oz. cranberry juice
1 oz. sugar

Mix all the ingredients in a blender for 10–15 seconds, or until smooth. Pour this mixture into the molds and place the molds in the freezer. When the mixture is partially frozen, stir the mixture in order to distribute the strawberries evenly throughout the pop.

Variation: For a *Raspberry-Cranberry Ice Pop*, substitute 6 ounces of raspberries for the strawberries. Proceed as directed above.

CHAPTER FIVE

Ice Pops Made
With Melons and Carrot Juice

In addition to the following recipes, feel free to make your own ice pops using single melons and carrot juice.

MELON DELIGHT ICE POP

This pinkish-orange pop is like a refreshing, summer punch.

4 oz. watermelon, sliced
2 oz. cantaloupe, sliced
2 oz. orange juice
2 oz. white (or Concord) grape juice
2 oz. banana, peeled and sliced

Mix all the ingredients in a blender for 10–15 seconds, or until smooth. Pour this mixture into the molds and place the molds in the freezer. When the mixture is partially frozen, stir the mixture in order to distribute the watermelon and cantaloupe evenly throughout the pop.

WATERMELON ICE POP

The tiny brown bits of cinnamon that are spread throughout this pinkish-red pop add just the right amount of spice to it—like a tangy, spicy watermelon ice on a stick. Perfect for summer!

10 oz. watermelon, sliced
 2 oz. lemon juice
 ¾ tsp. ground cinnamon

Mix all the ingredients in a blender for 10–15 seconds, or until smooth. Pour this mixture into the molds and place the molds in the freezer. When the mixture is partially frozen, stir the mixture in order to distribute the watermelon evenly throughout the pop.

CARROT-MILK ICE POP

With the sweetness of the carrot juice mixed with the creamy flavor of the milk, you can enjoy a couple of great alternating taste sensations as you consume this delicious, bright orange ice pop.

6 oz. carrot juice
6 oz. milk

Stir the ingredients together and pour this mixture into the molds. Place the molds in the freezer.

CARROT-PINEAPPLE ICE POP

Tangy, sweet pineapple juice mixed with the rich taste of carrot juice makes this a special ice pop.

8 oz. carrot juice
4 oz. pineapple juice

Stir the ingredients together and pour this mixture into the molds. Place the molds in the freezer. When the mixture is partially frozen, stir the mixture in order to distribute the juices evenly throughout the pop.

CARROT-YOGURT ICE POP I

If the yogurt seems a little bit sour in this pop, you may want to stir one teaspoon of sugar into the pop mixture before pouring the mixture into the molds.

6 oz. carrot juice
6 oz. plain yogurt

Stir the ingredients together until the mixture is smooth. Pour this mixture into the molds and place the molds in the freezer.

CARROT-YOGURT ICE POP II

The banana naturally sweetens this light orange ice pop and adds a special taste to the pop mixture.

6 oz. carrot juice
3 oz. plain yogurt
3 oz. banana, peeled and sliced

Mix all the ingredients in a blender for 10–15 seconds, or until smooth. Pour this mixture into the molds and place the molds in the freezer.

CARROT-APPLE ICE POP

This popular combination of fruit and vegetable juices is really like an ambrosia—and it's very healthy for you, whether in frozen or liquid form.

6 oz. carrot juice
6 oz. apple juice

Stir the ingredients together and pour this mixture into the molds. Place the molds in the freezer. When the mixture is partially frozen, stir the mixture in order to distribute the juices evenly throughout the pop.

Variation: For a stronger carrot taste with a hint of apple, use 8 ounces of carrot juice and 4 ounces of apple juice. Proceed as directed above.

CARROT-COCONUT ICE POP

Like a tropical treat with an earthy flavor, the tastes in this pop go back and forth from carrot to coconut and then back to carrot again—and at this ratio of juices, the tastes complement each other perfectly!

6 oz. carrot juice
6 oz. coconut juice

Stir the ingredients together and pour this mixture into the molds. Place the molds in the freezer.

CHAPTER SIX

Ice Pops Made
With Yogurts,
Puddings, and Sodas

In addition to the following recipes, feel free to make your own ice pops using single yogurts (e.g., vanilla, orange, peach, blueberry), puddings (e.g., chocolate, vanilla, butterscotch, pistachio), and sodas (e.g., cola, root beer, cream soda, cherry soda)—and any combinations thereof.

You can also add 3 ounces instant pudding mix to 9 ounces of any flavor of yogurt you desire (or to plain yogurt). Just stir the powder into the yogurt and spoon this mixture into the molds; then place the molds in the freezer.

In addition, you can mix 6 ounces of your favorite pudding (already prepared) with 6 ounces of any flavor of yogurt you desire (or with plain yogurt). Simply stir the ingredients together and spoon this mixture into the molds; then place the molds in the freezer.

CINNAMON-BROWN SUGAR
YOGURT POP

Cinnamon and brown sugar are old standards—why not use them in your yogurt pops?

¾ tsp. ground cinnamon
2 oz. brown sugar
12 oz. plain yogurt

Stir the cinnamon and brown sugar into the yogurt and spoon this mixture into the molds. Place the molds in the freezer.

MAPLE-BROWN SUGAR YOGURT POP

The maple syrup and brown sugar complement each other well in this yogurt pop.

 2 oz. maple syrup
 1 oz. brown sugar
12 oz. plain yogurt

Stir the maple syrup and brown sugar into the yogurt and spoon this mixture into the molds. Place the molds in the freezer.

PEACH-SPRINKLES YOGURT POP

This is a fun pop, as you mix the green, red, orange, yellow, pink, and blue sprinkles into the peach-colored yogurt. Besides, the sprinkles add a sweet taste to the pop from time to time.

 1 oz. sprinkles
12 oz. peach yogurt

Stir the sprinkles into the yogurt until the sprinkles are evenly spread throughout the pop mixture. Spoon this mixture into the molds and place the molds in the freezer.

Variations: Substitute your favorite yogurt (e.g., strawberry, banana, blueberry, or vanilla yogurt) for the peach yogurt and proceed as directed above.

VANILLA-CHOCOLATE YOGURT POP

Similar to the Vanilla-Chocolate Pudding Pop *(see page 86), the yogurt in this one gives it a tartness that creates its own special taste.*

1 oz. chocolate syrup
12 oz. vanilla yogurt

Stir the chocolate syrup into the yogurt just enough so that swirls of the chocolate syrup are visible throughout the pop mixture. Spoon this mixture into the molds and place the molds in the freezer.

Variation: For a *Coffee-Chocolate Yogurt Pop*, substitute 12 ounces of coffee yogurt for the vanilla yogurt and proceed as directed above.

STRAWBERRY-BANANA SWIRL YOGURT POP

This yogurt pop, in all of its variations, will look as good as it tastes.

6 oz. strawberry yogurt
6 oz. banana yogurt
1 tsp. sprinkles (optional)

Stir the strawberry yogurt, banana yogurt, and sprinkles together lightly, just enough so that swirls of the strawberry and banana yogurt are visible throughout the pop mixture. Spoon this mixture into the molds and place the molds in the freezer.

Variations: For red-and-blue swirls, substitute blueberry yogurt for the banana yogurt and proceed as directed above. For blue-and-yellow swirls, substitute blueberry yogurt for the strawberry yogurt and proceed as directed above.

BLUEBERRY-WALNUT YOGURT POP

The great taste of walnuts combines beautifully with the blueberry yogurt in this light purple pop.

3 oz. chopped walnuts
9 oz. blueberry yogurt

Stir the walnuts into the yogurt and spoon this mixture into the molds. Place the molds in the freezer.

Variations: For a *Blueberry-Almond Yogurt Pop*, substitute 3 ounces of chopped almonds for the walnuts and proceed as directed above. For a *Blueberry-Walnut-Raisin Yogurt Pop*, substitute 1 ounce of raisins for 1 ounce of the walnuts (or almonds) and proceed as directed above.

RASPBERRY-VANILLA-RASPBERRY YOGURT POP

This red-and-white concoction allows you to experience the delicious taste of raspberry at the top and the bottom of the pop.

8 oz. raspberry yogurt
4 oz. vanilla yogurt

Fill ⅓ of each mold with raspberry yogurt, the next ⅓ with vanilla yogurt, and the final ⅓ with raspberry yogurt. Place the molds in the freezer.

Variations: Substitute 8 ounces of blueberry, strawberry, peach, or cherry yogurt for the raspberry yogurt and proceed as directed above.

FOURTH OF JULY YOGURT POP

You may want to stir ½ teaspoon of sprinkles into the strawberry yogurt in each of these red-white-and-blue pops.

4 oz. strawberry yogurt
4 oz. vanilla yogurt
4 oz. blueberry yogurt

Fill ⅓ of each mold with strawberry yogurt, the next ⅓ with vanilla yogurt, and the final ⅓ with blueberry yogurt. Place the molds in the freezer.

CUSTARD ICE POP

Feel free to make this yellow ice pop without the nutmeg, if you desire. Either way, it's a real tasty frozen treat on a stick.

12 oz. vanilla custard
⅜ tsp. ground nutmeg

Stir the ingredients together and spoon this mixture into the molds. Place the molds in the freezer.

VANILLA PUDDING ICE POP

A pale yellow pop with light brown specks of cinnamon and nutmeg, the key to this one is the raisins, which are slowly revealed as you consume the pop.

9 oz. vanilla pudding
3 oz. raisins
⅜ tsp. ground cinnamon
⅜ tsp. ground nutmeg

Stir all the ingredients together and spoon this mixture into the molds. Place the molds in the freezer.

VANILLA-CHOCOLATE PUDDING POP

Two popular puddings share the stage in this ice pop, creating a whole that is at least as good as the two parts— if not better.

6 oz. chocolate pudding
6 oz. vanilla pudding

Stir the chocolate pudding into the vanilla pudding just enough so that swirls of the chocolate pudding are visible throughout the pop mixture. Spoon this mixture into the molds and place the molds in the freezer.

PISTACHIO-LEMON PUDDING POP

Whether you use the sprinkles or not, this green-and-yellow pop is sure to satisfy.

6 oz. pistachio pudding
6 oz. lemon pudding
1 tsp. sprinkles (optional)

Stir the pistachio pudding, lemon pudding, and sprinkles together lightly, just enough so that swirls of the pistachio and lemon pudding are visible throughout the pop mixture. Spoon this mixture into the molds and place the molds in the freezer.

Variation: For a *Pistachio-Vanilla Pudding Pop*, substitute 6 ounces of vanilla pudding for the lemon pudding and proceed as directed above.

STRAWBERRY-LEMON PUDDING POP

The frozen strawberries and pieces of banana melt in your mouth—great treats!

  2 oz. strawberries, sliced
10 oz. lemon pudding

Stir the strawberries into the pudding and spoon this mixture into the molds. Place the molds in the freezer.

Variations: For a *Banana-Lemon Pudding Pop*, substitute 2 ounces of peeled and sliced banana for the strawberries and proceed as directed above. You may also wish to use 1 ounce each of the strawberries and banana.

CHOCOLATE PUDDING ICE POP

The tan-and-brown walnuts that are embedded in this chocolate-colored pop are as inviting to the eye as they are to the taste buds.

3 oz. chopped walnuts
9 oz. chocolate pudding

Stir the walnuts into the pudding and spoon this mixture into the molds. Place the molds in the freezer.

BUTTERSCOTCH-CHOCOLATE-VANILLA PUDDING POP

This pop enables you to enjoy three of the greatest tastes of all time—in the same place!

4 oz. butterscotch pudding
4 oz. chocolate pudding
4 oz. vanilla pudding

Fill ⅓ of each mold with butterscotch pudding, the next ⅓ with chocolate pudding, and the final ⅓ with vanilla pudding. Place the molds in the freezer.

VANILLA-CHERRY SODA
PUDDING POP

The taste of vanilla is enhanced by a hint of cherry in these pops.

4 oz. cherry soda
8 oz. vanilla pudding

Stir the soda into the pudding and pour this mixture into the molds. Place the molds in the freezer.

Variation: Substitute 4 ounces of grape soda for the cherry soda and proceed as directed above.

BUTTERSCOTCH-ROOT BEER PUDDING POP

This unlikely combination of ingredients actually produces a fantastic ice pop which tastes mostly of butterscotch, with a hint of root beer.

4 oz. root beer
8 oz. butterscotch pudding

Stir the root beer into the pudding and pour this mixture into the molds. Place the molds in the freezer.

COLA-CHERRY SODA POP

Add a hint of cherry—or substitute orange or grape—flavor to your cola pops.

8 oz. cola
4 oz. cherry soda

Stir the ingredients together and pour this mixture into the molds. Place the molds in the freezer.

ROOT BEER-CREAM SODA POP

The vanilla taste of cream soda and the unique taste of root beer mix well with each other.

6 oz. root beer
6 oz. cream soda

Stir the ingredients together and pour this mixture into the molds. Place the molds in the freezer.

Variations: Substitute 6 ounces of cola for the cream soda or the root beer, and proceed as directed above.

LEMON-LIME-GRAPE SODA POP

This pop will be purple, white, or orange—depending on which variation you use.

6 oz. lemon-lime soda
6 oz. grape soda

Stir the ingredients together and pour this mixture into the molds. Place the molds in the freezer.

Variations: Substitute 6 ounces of ginger ale or orange soda for the grape soda and proceed as directed above.

CREAM SODA-ROOT BEER-COLA POP

What can you say about the flavors that are combined in this pop—delicious!

4 oz. cream soda
4 oz. root beer
4 oz. cola

Stir all the ingredients together and pour this mixture into the molds. Place the molds in the freezer.

CHERRY-ORANGE-GRAPE SODA POP

This pop is like having a fruit punch on a stick!

4 oz. cherry soda
4 oz. orange soda
4 oz. grape soda

Stir all the ingredients together and pour this mixture into the molds. Place the molds in the freezer.

CHAPTER SEVEN

Ice Pops Made
With Chocolate, Coffee,
Tea, Nuts, and Candies

In addition to the following recipes, feel free to make your own ice pops using your favorite flavors, nuts, candies, and any other sweet ingredients you desire.

CHOCOLATE-MINT ICE POP

This chocolate-colored pop is like a minty "Fudgesicle." Feel free to make this one without the mint extract, if you desire. Either way, it's a great chocolate experience.

12 oz. milk
 2 oz. chocolate syrup
¾ tsp. mint extract

Stir all the ingredients together and pour this mixture into the molds. Place the molds in the freezer.

CAPPUCCINO ICE POP

The distinctive tastes of chocolate and espresso alternate between each other in this delicious, dark brown pop. It might even help wake you up in the morning!

6 oz. freshly made espresso
6 oz. milk
2 oz. chocolate syrup

Stir all the ingredients together and pour this mixture into the molds. Place the molds in the freezer.

Variation: Substitute 1 ounce sugar for the chocolate syrup. Proceed as directed above.

TEA ICE POP

This off-white pop tastes like a frozen cup of Earl Grey tea on a stick—believe it or not!

6 oz. freshly made Earl Grey (or another orange pekoe)
  tea
6 oz. milk
1 oz. sugar (optional)

Stir all the ingredients together and pour this mixture into the molds. Place the molds in the freezer.

TOASTED ALMOND ICE POP

The ground almonds serve as a great background flavor for this pop, while the toasted almonds add a toasty, almond taste to the pop—like the Good Humor bar of the same name that you had as a kid. Feel free to toast the ground almonds too, if you wish (for 3–5 minutes at 350°F).

3 oz. chopped almonds
3 oz. ground almonds
1 oz. sugar
6 oz. milk

Place the chopped almonds in the oven for 5–10 minutes at 350°F, or until the almonds are a toasty brown color. Stir these almonds (along with the ground almonds and the sugar) into the milk in a bowl and place the bowl in the freezer for 1–2 hours, or until the mixture is partially frozen. Stir the mixture again to spread the almonds evenly throughout the milk, and spoon this mixture into the molds. Place the molds in the freezer.

HAZELNUT ICE POP

This pop has sweet pieces of hazelnut throughout that serve as rewards.

3 oz. chopped hazelnuts
1 oz. sugar
¾ tsp. vanilla extract
9 oz. milk

Stir the hazelnuts, sugar, and vanilla extract into the milk in a bowl and place the bowl in the freezer for 1–2 hours, or until the mixture is partially frozen. Stir the mixture again to spread the hazelnuts evenly throughout the milk, and spoon this mixture into the molds. Place the molds in the freezer.

Variation: Substitute 3 ounces of ground hazelnuts for the chopped hazelnuts. Proceed as directed above.

PECAN ICE POP

Like butter pecan ice cream, this pop is made all the richer by the use of the brown sugar—a real treat!

3 oz. chopped pecans
1 oz. brown sugar
¾ tsp. vanilla extract
9 oz. milk

Stir the pecans, brown sugar, and vanilla extract into the milk in a bowl and place the bowl in the freezer for 1–2 hours, or until the mixture is partially frozen. Stir the mixture again to spread the pecans evenly throughout the milk, and spoon this mixture into the molds. Place the molds in the freezer.

PEANUT BUTTER–CHOCOLATE
ICE POP

This pop is truly unique—but for peanut butter lovers, it's a real treat. You can make this one with either smooth or chunky peanut butter.

 2 oz. chocolate syrup
12 oz. peanut butter

Stir the chocolate syrup into the peanut butter just enough so that swirls of the chocolate syrup are visible throughout the pop mixture. Spoon this mixture into the molds and place the molds in the freezer.

VANILLA ICE POP

This pop is like having a vanilla milkshake on a stick—one of the best tastes of all time!

1 oz. sugar
¾ tsp. vanilla extract
12 oz. milk

Stir all the ingredients together and pour this mixture into the molds. Place the molds in the freezer.

MAPLE ICE POP

Whether you use the maple syrup or the honey, this ice pop is like having a frozen piece of candy on a stick—great for dessert!

12 oz. milk
1 oz. maple syrup
¾ tsp. vanilla extract

Stir all the ingredients together and pour this mixture into the molds. Place the molds in the freezer.

Variation: For a *Honey Ice Pop*, substitute 1 ounce of honey for the maple syrup and vanilla extract. Proceed as directed above.

PEPPERMINT CANDY ICE POP

The more you stir the candy, the more the peppermint taste will sink into the milk—and the pinker the pop becomes!

1 oz. peppermint candy
¾ tsp. vanilla extract
11 oz. milk

Break the peppermint candy up into small pieces. Stir the candy and the vanilla extract into the milk in a bowl and place the bowl in the freezer for 1–2 hours, or until the mixture is partially frozen. Stir the mixture again to spread the candy evenly throughout the milk, and spoon this mixture into the molds. Place the molds in the freezer.

PEANUT BRITTLE ICE POP

Let's face it—there's nothing like peanut brittle! The more you stir this one, the more the caramel taste will sink into the milk.

6 oz. peanut brittle
6 oz. milk

Break the peanut brittle up into small pieces. Stir the peanut brittle into the milk in a bowl and place the bowl in the freezer for 1–2 hours, or until the mixture is partially frozen. Stir the mixture again to spread the peanut brittle evenly throughout the milk, and spoon this mixture into the molds. Place the molds in the freezer.

Variation: For a *Peanut Ice Pop*, substitute 6 ounces of unsalted, roasted peanuts (chopped, if desired) and 1 ounce of sugar for the peanut brittle. Proceed as directed above.

CHAPTER EIGHT

Ice Pops Made With Liquor

In addition to the following recipes (for adults), feel free to make your own ice pops using your favorite liquors along with any other ingredients you think might go well with them. Salut!

ORANGE-COINTREAU ICE POP

Orange juice and orange liqueur—a great combination!

11 oz. orange juice
1 oz. Cointreau (or Grand Marnier)

Stir the ingredients together and pour this mixture into the molds. Place the molds in the freezer.

SANGRIA ICE POP

*A dark, rose-colored pop, this one has enough tangy juices
in it to keep your taste buds snapping—sangria on a stick.*

5 oz. orange juice
1 oz. lemon juice
1 oz. lime juice
4 oz. pineapple juice
1 oz. red wine

   Stir all the ingredients together and pour this mixture into
the molds. Place the molds in the freezer.

ORANGE-GRAPEFRUIT COCKTAIL ICE POP

A yellow pop with a faint hint of orange in it, this one's a citrus, tropical cocktail treat—perfect for the Caribbean.

6 oz. orange juice
5 oz. grapefruit juice
½ oz. rum
½ oz. brandy

Stir all the ingredients together and pour this mixture into the molds. Place the molds in the freezer.

ORANGE-GRAPE PUNCH ICE POP

With white grape juice, this punchy pop is orange-colored with a light, wine taste; with Concord grape juice, it's purple with a heavier taste, much like sangria.

5 oz. orange juice
4 oz. white (or Concord) grape juice
2 oz. lemon juice
1 oz. white wine

Stir all the ingredients together and pour this mixture into the molds. Place the molds in the freezer.

APRICOT-RUM ICE POP

This one's a yellowish-orange pop; the apricot and the rum tastes work together well.

6 oz. apricots, peeled and sliced
5 oz. pineapple juice
1 oz. rum

Mix all the ingredients in a blender for 10–15 seconds, or until smooth. Pour this mixture into the molds and place the molds in the freezer.

APPLE-RUM ICE POP

This light brown pop will remind you of a crisp autumn day with a cup of spiked apple cider in your hand!

11 oz. apple juice
1 oz. rum

Stir the ingredients together and pour this mixture into the molds. Place the molds in the freezer.

PINEAPPLE-CRANBERRY COCKTAIL ICE POP

Tart from the cranberry and sweet from the pineapple, this light purple pop would be good for summer cocktail hour at the beach.

6 oz. pineapple juice
5 oz. cranberry juice
1 oz. vodka

Stir all the ingredients together and pour this mixture into the molds. Place the molds in the freezer.

PINEAPPLE-COCONUT DELIGHT ICE POP

The addition of the grenadine turns this whitish-yellow pop into a yellowish-pink one that is a tiny bit sweeter than the original. Either way, it's a nice, exotic treat.

6 oz. pineapple juice
5 oz. coconut juice
1 oz. amaretto
¾ tsp. grenadine (optional)

Stir all the ingredients together and pour this mixture into the molds. Place the molds in the freezer. When the mixture is partially frozen, stir the mixture in order to distribute the juices evenly throughout the pop.

Variation: Substitute ½ ounce of amaretto and ½ ounce of rum for the amaretto. Proceed as directed above.

PAPAYA-PINEAPPLE COCKTAIL ICE POP

What an amazing assortment of tastes you will have in this orangish-yellow pop—a tropical treat on a stick!

4⅔ oz. papaya, peeled and sliced
4 oz. pineapple juice
2⅔ oz. orange juice
⅔ oz. rum

Mix all the ingredients in a blender for 10–15 seconds, or until smooth. Pour this mixture into the molds and place the molds in the freezer.

BANANA-COCONUT DAIQUIRI
ICE POP

The tastes of coconut, banana, and pineapple dominate this pinkish-red pop—with the hint of rum giving it just the richness it needs.

3 oz. coconut juice
3 oz. pineapple juice
2 oz. strawberries, sliced
3 oz. banana, peeled and sliced
1 oz. rum

Mix all the ingredients in a blender for 10–15 seconds, or until smooth. Pour this mixture into the molds and place the molds in the freezer.

RASPBERRY-COINTREAU ICE POP

The less sugar you use, the more tart this dark red pop will be—but it's still pretty sweet without the sugar.

11 oz. raspberries
1 oz. Cointreau (or Grand Marnier)
½ oz. sugar (optional)

Mix all the ingredients in a blender for 10–15 seconds, or until smooth. Pour this mixture into the molds and place the molds in the freezer.

Variation: For a *Strawberry-Cointreau Ice Pop*, substitute 11 ounces of sliced strawberries for the raspberries. Proceed as directed above.

STRAWBERRY DAIQUIRI ICE POP

The lime in this pop gives it a tangy taste that mixes well with the rum.

9 oz. strawberries, sliced
2 oz. lime juice
1 oz. rum

Mix all the ingredients in a blender for 10–15 seconds, or until smooth. Pour this mixture into the molds and place the molds in the freezer.

STRAWBERRY PIÑA COLADA
ICE POP

Imagine that you are on a distant South Sea Island as you're sucking on this pinkish-red pop, and transport yourself to a faraway world.

5 oz. strawberries, sliced
2 oz. coconut juice
4 oz. pineapple juice
1 oz. rum

Mix all the ingredients in a blender for 10–15 seconds, or until smooth. Pour this mixture into the molds and place the molds in the freezer.

BLUEBERRY MINT JULEP ICE POP

Try this dark purple pop on a hot New Orleans day while sitting in Jackson Square—or anywhere else, for that matter.

11 oz. blueberries
 1 oz. bourbon
⅜ tsp. mint extract

Mix all the ingredients in a blender for 10–15 seconds, or until smooth. Pour this mixture into the molds and place the molds in the freezer.

BLUEBERRY-RUM COCKTAIL
ICE POP

If you have to add anything to the great taste of blueberries, a little bit of rum and grenadine certainly does the trick.

11 oz. blueberries
1 oz. rum
¾ tsp. grenadine

Mix all the ingredients in a blender for 10–15 seconds, or until smooth. Pour this mixture into the molds and place the molds in the freezer.

CANTALOUPE-RUM ICE POP

You might want to substitute honeydew melon for the cantaloupe in this one, and you also might want to add a little bit of honey to the pop mixture before blending it up, in order to sweeten the pop just a bit.

6 oz. cantaloupe, peeled and sliced
1 oz. orange juice
4 oz. strawberries, sliced
1 oz. rum

Mix all the ingredients in a blender for 10–15 seconds, or until smooth. Pour this mixture into the molds and place the molds in the freezer.

WATERMELON COCKTAIL ICE POP

*The pineapple juice spices this one up, as does the rum.
If there's such a thing as a watermelon cocktail, this is
it.*

6 oz. watermelon, sliced
2 oz. orange juice
2 oz. pineapple juice
1 oz. strawberries, sliced
1 oz. rum

Mix all the ingredients in a blender for 10–15 seconds,
or until smooth. Pour this mixture into the molds and place
the molds in the freezer.

CARROT-CRÈME DE CACAO ICE POP

The experience of sucking on this pop is nothing short of incredible, as the crème de cacao (or Kahlúa) melts first and fills your mouth with its sweet flavor, followed by the milky carrot juice.

   4 oz. milk
1 ⅓ oz. crème de cacao
6 ⅔ oz. carrot juice
   ½ tsp. ground cinnamon (optional)

Stir all the ingredients together and pour this mixture into the molds. Place the molds in the freezer.

Variation: For a *Carrot-Kahlúa Ice Pop*, substitute 1 ⅓ ounces of Kahlúa for the crème de cacao. Proceed as directed above.

COINTREAU ICE POP

The subtle taste of Cointreau becomes evident in this pop as you suck on it—like a dessert in itself.

11 oz. milk
 1 oz. Cointreau (or Grand Marnier)

Stir the ingredients together and pour this mixture into the molds. Place the molds in the freezer.

PEAR-RED WINE ICE POP

The white pieces of pear in this rose-colored pop are a special treat—like a pear-wine punch on a stick.

6 oz. pear, peeled and sliced
1 oz. red wine
4 oz. orange juice
1 oz. lemon juice

Mix all the ingredients in a blender for 10–15 seconds, or until smooth. Pour this mixture into the molds and place the molds in the freezer. When the mixture is partially frozen, stir the mixture in order to distribute the wine and pear evenly throughout the pop.

PISTACHIO-CHARTREUSE ICE POP

This herby-minty liqueur adds an extra zing to the pudding, which has little bits of pistachio nuts in it. Feel free to add unsalted, roasted pistachio nuts (chopped, if desired) to the light green pop mixture.

1 oz. green Chartreuse
11 oz. pistachio pudding

Stir the Chartreuse into the pudding and spoon this mixture into the molds. Place the molds in the freezer.

BLOODY MARY ICE POP

Whether you like your Bloody Mary simple (as in the variation) or spicy, this pop will satisfy your desire to taste a popular cocktail in a frozen form.

10 oz. unsalted tomato juice
 1 oz. vodka
 1 oz. lemon juice
 ¾ tsp. Worcestershire sauce
 ⅛ tsp. salt (optional)
 ⅛ tsp. pepper (optional)

Stir all the ingredients together and pour this mixture into the molds. Place the molds in the freezer.

Variation: For a *Tomato-Vodka Ice Pop*, substitute 11 ounces of unsalted tomato juice and 1 ounce of vodka for this recipe. Proceed as directed above.

KIWI-COINTREAU ICE POP

The unique, tangy-sweet taste of kiwi fruit blends well with the orange liqueur in this olive-green pop.

10 oz. kiwi fruit, peeled and sliced
 2 oz. Cointreau (or Grand Marnier)

Mix the ingredients in a blender for 10–15 seconds, or until smooth. Spoon this mixture into the molds and place the molds in the freezer.

DIRECTORY

Where to Get

Ice-Pop Molds

Tupperware
World Headquarters
Post Office Box 2353
Orlando, FL 32802

Sets of six 2-ounce plastic Ice Tups molds are available by mail order and from local Tupperware consultants.

Arrow Plastic Manufacturing Company
701 East Devon Avenue
Elk Grove, IL 60007

Plastic molds make four or eight 2-ounce pops, or four 3-ounce pops, and are available at supermarkets and other stores across the country.

James River Corporation
Consumer Products Business
Post Office Box 6000
RiverPark
Norwalk, CT 06856

3- and 5-ounce Dixie cups are available at supermarkets and other stores across the country.